TRUMP CAN WIN IN 2020

Michael Brackman

TRUMP CAN WIN IN 2020
ALL RIGHTS RESERVED.
COPYRIGHT © 2020 Michael Brackman

The content of this book is the sole expression, belief and opinion of its author based on his observations and not that of the publisher or editor. No warranties or guarantees are expressed or implied by the publisher's choice to include any of the content in this volume. Neither the publisher, editor, nor the individual author shall be liable for any physical, psychological, emotional, financial, or commercial damages, including, but not limited to, special, incidental, consequential, or other damages. Our views and rights are the same -- you are responsible for your own choices, actions, and results.

Publisher: Absolute Author Publishing House
Editor: Dr. Melissa Caudle

ISBN: 978-1-64953-012-7

DEDICATION

To my great mother, Perma, who had the courage to want more and came to America so that we could have an education. Thank you for believing in me when I did not believe the greatness within.

To our great founding fathers, who, in their wisdom, designed a democracy for us to follow.

ACKNOWLEDGMENT

My associates, Gillian and Gina, have been instrumental in getting this piece out, and their contributions are much appreciated.

TABLE OF CONTENTS

PREFACE	i
Chapter 1	1
Trumpnosis	1
Chapter 2	6
Coming Forward With my Secret Tools	6
Chapter 3	9
Trump's Self-Serving Loyalty	9
Chapter 4	13
Look Closely	13
Chapter 5	18
Modeling	18
Chapter 6	22
Is Artificial Intelligence	22
Influencing Man?	22
Chapter 7	36

Questionable Behavior 36

Chapter 8 52

Path of Least Resistance 52

Chapter 9 57

Continuing Down This Road 57

Chapter 10 69

Our Fear of Becoming the Minority Race
.... 69

Chapter 11 77

Trump's Undying Love Affair with Dictators.. 77

Chapter 12 86

Pay Attention (Or Less of It).................. 86

Epilogue 96

ABOUT THE AUTHOR 100

Glossary 114

Reference List... 118

INDEX... 120

PREFACE

In the early months of 1997, my friend, Gregory Howard, called excited to tell me about a seminar that could propel my life to the next level. He knew I was always game for a challenge and was very surprised that I had never heard of a famous Guru who, for this book, I will call Thomas. Gregory always had news of the latest self-improvement training, and so we would run off in search of more profound knowledge and constant self-improvement. I admired his tenacity from a distance.

Later that week, after talking to Greg in length, I met a man in the grocery store who struck up an impromptu conversation with me while we waited our turn in the long checkout line. The next thing I know, he was telling me how much Guru Thomas had changed his life forever. I looked at him and paused; this must be synchronicity. When more than one person tells you the same thing, it is time to action what you have been told. From that point on, I knew that I was soon to be on an airplane to meet the famous Thomas in person for myself. This guru delivered in the fullest, and my life is better for it.

As fate would have it, I was to meet a Swedish gentleman named Claudio Sennhauser, who has since become a very good friend and fellow neurolinguistic programming (NLP) practitioner. Claudio had spent several years studying beside the cofounder of NLP technology, Doctor Richard Bandler. Claudio sat down thoughtfully one day and softly asked me, "Why not study with the headmaster?"

I looked at him pensively and felt his words resonated in my soul. So in 1997, I went to London, England. Mind you, since then, I have been honored to study with many leading master hypnotists and experts in similar fields.

Over the next two decades, I would continue to return to work for and participate in Thomas' events over the years. Thomas has coached many celebrities out there and at least one President. I have been in close proximity with them all, including, yes, you have guessed it, Mr. Trump himself.

Michael Brackman

Michael Brackman

Chapter 1
Trumpnosis

We ought to aspire to use our own free will as people rather than be SHEEPLE. My name is Michael Brackman, and I have been studying the strategies of influence in the subject of neuro-linguistic programming (NLP) and Ericksonian Hypnosis since around 1997 with one of Trump's mentors/teachers. Trump has since been in close proximity to many of our fellow students/mentees.

TRUMP CAN WIN IN 2020

I cannot genuinely say Trump has absorbed the teachings because he admits he does not read or even knows American history or civics for that matter. He may have natural instincts, although I can say with a high degree of certainty that he is coached. All fellow students of this art of influence are encouraged to have coaching by our mutual teacher/mentor or by someone on his team, which is where it began for me around that same year.

There is a smorgasbord of techniques, and I can't see Trump learning and practicing them because his attention span is too short, and I don't believe he has the discipline it takes to practice to become proficient with such a vast array of techniques.

Perhaps by the time you finish this book, you will have a little more insight into the man himself, and maybe you will even find a few things that make him a winner worth modeling. However, I would not model any of the unflattering antics he displays to distract the conscious mind.

There is a term going around that I may have to borrow from Richard Barker called "Trumpnosis." I will call what Trump does "Trumpnosis Patterns." The techniques are magical and work even when we are aware of what is going on, although now it is starting to appear more and more that is just madness. Perhaps he does not have the discipline to be coached as lately; he only appears to be off the rails and completely out of control.

Normally when a skilled hypnotist or NLP practitioner, appears crazed, it is purposeful to reach the client's unconscious by distracting the conscious mind.

Nevertheless, Trump has become a phenomenon in every sense of the word defying all odds. In all fairness, if you were to meet him and be a witness to his spell, he would probably charm your pants off you. He is extremely charismatic and engages those he meets; and not necessarily for the good.

TRUMP CAN WIN IN 2020

My aim is to show you the magic of Trump and Trumpnosis. In January 2016, at a campaign rally in Iowa, Trump said, "I could stand in the middle of Fifth Avenue and shoot somebody, and I wouldn't lose voters."

Displaying absolute certainty, along with humor, is an essential aspect of this technology, although there are times when a subordinate stance is useful.

One of my most recent and dearest teachers in the "Master Mind Group" group I participate in, insists that we commit to integrity because it's a very personal and powerful relationship to get into another's mind and heart.

That, for me, is first and foremost, and we go first into a trance, meaning, to enter another one's private world, we must first go into a trance ourselves.

I have believed from early on that these powerful tools should never be given to the irresponsible and unethical, and that same Mastermind teacher teaches that it is to be used only as "a force for Good."

Watch out for the 2020 contenders!

Chapter 2

Coming Forward With my Secret Tools

I feel compelled to divulge these secret tools now because I can see how President Trump masterfully took us all, from elite scholars to his "chosen ones" in the Rust Belt, on the exact journey he wanted us to go on.

We are all guilty of giving him what he wants most: our undivided attention. We must admit, it is interesting how he PURPOSEFULLY GUIDES us all. He may continue to do that if given a second term. The only difference is that he would be more confident and emboldened than ever.

You see, he never believed he would win despite all of the alleged help from Russia. There were many desperate moves during his 2016 campaign, coupled with many Hail Mary's. According to Trump's friend Howard Stern in a CNN interview, "This was a PUBLICITY stunt." Donald Trump apparently never intended to be President. Yet here we are.

Then FBI Director, James Comey's, last-minute blunder, announcing he was restarting the Hillary Clinton email investigation days before the election, along with the fact that many Black and Brown Democrats simply assumed Hillary would win and stayed home, are the reasons we find ourselves where we are now. All of this was the intention of the social media chaos caused by the alleged Russian disinformation campaign.

TRUMP CAN WIN IN 2020

Admittedly, I too was manipulated and remained inactive. I almost did not make it to the polls myself. I neglected to participate in the door-to-door efforts to drive people to the polls as I had in 2008. I assumed we would have a better-qualified president holding the highest office. Unfortunately, this did not come to pass.

I am hoping to shed some light on several ways Trump masterfully and purposefully took us where he wanted us to go. I hope all my years of quietly obsessing about the human mind will help you make wise and informed decisions when the next election rolls around.

Chapter 3

Trump's Self-Serving Loyalty

Trump claims to follow his instincts, and admittedly, there is a lot to be said about instincts. I follow my inner guidance system, and I innately know when it is time to move away from or towards a project. However, I do not know if instinct alone is enough to hold the highest office of the world's most powerful nation. In Trump's case, we are dealing with a powerful, self-serving, narcissistic man/boy.

TRUMP CAN WIN IN 2020

It is safe to say that Trump is not loyal. Everyone knows he deserted his late friend, Roy Cohn, who passed away on August 2, 1986, from an AIDS-related illness at the age of fifty-nine.

According to *Vanity Fair*, "With the ruthless attorney and guide Roy Cohn, Trump propelled himself into the city's power circles." Cohn is best known for his involvement with the rise and fall of the dark political era of McCarthyism. Victor A. Kovner, a lawyer who knew Cohn for many years, stated, "You knew when you were in Cohn's presence, you were in the presence of PURE EVIL."

Rumors abound that Cohn helped Trump deal with many legal entanglements without charging a penny. Cohn taught Trump how to rise to fame with an intense and unapologetic bravado; to play the game, so to speak. Cohn stood by Trump through thick and thin, much like his recent attorney, Michael Cohen, who is currently serving prison time for tax and campaign finance crimes.

In 1978, Trump was so grateful to Cohn for winning a seemingly impossible legal battle, at no charge once again, that he gifted Cohn diamond-encrusted cuff links and buttons in a Bulgari box as a symbol of his gratitude.

After his death, it is said that Cohn's partner, Peter Fraser, got the cuff links and buttons appraised only to be told they were complete knock-offs.

It is rumored that after losing all his money, with hardly a shirt left on his back, Cohn asked Trump for a place to lay his head during his last days. Trump reluctantly gave him a leftover, hardly livable corner in one of his buildings.

Shocked by the betrayal, Cohn later said, as quoted in late journalist Wayne Barrett's 1992 book about Trump, "Donald pisses ice water."

TRUMP CAN WIN IN 2020

The only person that has gotten the best of Trump was his ex-wife, Ivana Trump, although not without a fight.

Trump divorced Ivana after meeting Marla Maples, with whom he began an affair in the early 90s.

By then, Trump had learned his lesson and divorced Marla shortly before the five-year prenup expired. This was often a joke in our training.

Chapter 4

Look Closely

Most of Trump's antics were purposeful; make no mistake about it. With the help of Cambridge Analytica, Trump was able to target his subjects and turn them into raving fans easily. This is an important lesson we learned from our mentor, "Create a raving fan base and innovate, innovate, innovate," he would say.

Now, let's talk about the Colin Kaepernick incident. How can anyone forget about this?

TRUMP CAN WIN IN 2020

We witnessed Trump verbally attaching and condescending Colin Kaepernick for peacefully protesting on the football field. Nike responded to the verbosity by hiring Kaepernick as their spokesperson, and as a result, Nike stocks shot up, and suddenly there was no more mention of Kaepernick by Trump.

I would not at all be surprised if Trump owns stocks in Nike. For him, it's all about winning and personal gain, no matter where it comes from.

I would not attempt to psychoanalyze Trump in a million years, but another training tool I briefly studied, way before I began to study hypnosis, was the Enneagram. From the Enneagram point of view, I would say Trump wants to be loved or is classified as what is termed as an achiever. The wanting to be loved personality type, learned around the age of five, stems from learning which side of the bread the butter is on, so to speak. That is to say, they know who has the power and whom they need to please.

Wanting to be loved personality types derive their value from performing to please the masculine energy.

Somehow, the wanting to be loved receives the message that to get the love, they must manipulate or cajole others. If that does not work, they will get the hammer and attempt to use that as strength or as a compelling argument, and if that still does not work, they will pull out the Uzi such as in Trump's late-night Twitter storms. That is to say, this type of personality will go to any lengths to manipulate and thus get what they want, which in my opinion, is the unhealthy wanting to be loved personality type.

The achiever, on the other hand, tends to be very vain. They need the best car, the hottest women, or men on their arm, and they tend to become very successful. In their disintegration or today known as an unhealthy achiever, however, they revert to success by any means necessary. They become relentless about destroying whatever reminds them of their shortcomings and failures, psychopathic behavior, and can correspond to the narcissistic personality disorder. In other words, if they cannot be the best business person, attorney, or even the President, they will settle for being the best criminal. They have to win at any cost.

The achiever personality type learned early on that they needed to get the love from performing.

The Enneagram is a system of classifying personality types, and it has been around since ancient times, though its origin has never been established. Lately, it has become a hot topic among Evangelicals.

The Enneagram has been quite a precise tool over the years. It has been decades since I revived my familiarity with the Enneagram; however, I don't believe Trump has ever reached integration or healthy growth. We are all on a continuum on our personality spectrums. At any given time, we can integrate or disintegrate into different levels on that continuum. Most highly conscious beings tend to rise to integration as we raise our vibration. This is not without work. That is why we must be conscious. Based on the Enneagram, he appears to be an unhealthy achiever, with some arguing he is beyond sociopathy.

I would say, take a close look at Donald Trump.

Chapter 5

Modeling

Modeling is another critical NLP tool. It merely means to model behavior to achieve excellence by mastering the beliefs, physiology, and way of thinking of the person whom you would like to model.

I would venture to say it was the core teachings of Dr. Richard Bandler and John Grinder, cofounders of NLP. They began to study and model Doctor Milton Erickson, a psychiatrist, who specialized in medical hypnosis in the 70s. According to Lansiedel NLP training in 1977, they developed the Milton Model.

That said, we tend to naturally model the behavior of our parents or those who most influence us as children.

One could say that matching and mirroring is a form of modeling in its simplistic form. Still, the umbrella of modeling is vast and much more complicated than merely mirroring and matching, which is what I refer to as the kindergarten NLP.

According to Robert Dilts, another colossal figure in the NLP community, "NLP is the process with which the relevant behavioral components of those communicatively gifted people were discovered and organized into a working model (source and fact check- Landsiedel NLP training).

Taking a peek at Donald Trump Junior's mannerism at rallies, I would say that he models his father, the music played is the same they play when Donald

TRUMP CAN WIN IN 2020

Senior is walking on stage, This is called an anchor, which I will cover later. Notice that they start with the yes factor, which is having the audience get used to saying yes. It's a typical agreement technique. The way it is done is by making verifiable statements, then seamlessly leaning into what they want the subjects to accept as facts.

Of course, I repeat, I would not even begin to suggest that Trump Senior or Junior have learned any of these tools. What I will say, once again, is that I can guess with a considerable degree of certainty is that they are all being coached, and that may include many of his staff as that is customarily encouraged within the NLP community of our great mentor, Thomas.

Generally speaking, we can mark out what we want to install in the unconscious with dramatic gestures or we can do what we call spatial anchoring, where we use a specific spot for specific commands or tonality can also be used.

Michael Brackman

I must admit that I would be highly disappointed if it is our mutual teacher Thomas, Trump's friend, and our mutual mentor, that is giving him lessons because I consider my teacher to be of high integrity.

Also, I must add that 2020 contenders may want to avoid modeling his least attractive behaviors. But some of his strategies are worth paying attention to, or at least recognizing if only to inoculate themselves against being under Trump's spell.

Chapter 6

Is Artificial Intelligence Influencing Man?

So exactly how did some become the selected Chosen Ones? Hypnosis is a specialized method of influencing the unconscious. It is defined as the focus of one thing at the exclusion of all others. To do that, one must distract the conscious mind and influence the unconscious mind.

Michael Brackman

In addition to NLP, Trump not only used hypnosis masterfully during the 2016 election campaign, but he also received an enormous boost from Cambridge Analytica.

Cambridge Analytica was created in 2013 by Nigel Oakes. It was the offshoot of Strategic Communications Laboratories (SCL) in London, a behavioral research company.

In 2014, John Rust, a professor at the University of Cambridge, saw the potential danger in Cambridge Analytica's massive data-mining efforts, and he warned the university. According to an email reviewed by *WIRED*, "Rust informed the university that one of the school's psychology professors, Aleksander Kogan, was using an app he created to collect data on millions of Facebook users without their knowledge."

TRUMP CAN WIN IN 2020

This app not only collected data on the individuals who used the app but also collected data on all their friends. "Their intention," wrote Rust, "is to extend this to the entire U.S. population and use it within an election campaign." Kogan's client was a little-known political campaign company that became none other than Cambridge Analytica.

As director of the university's Psychometrics Center, Rust had a thorough understanding of how this data could be used. With forty years of experience, Rust saw how these types of data could be used to form the basis of SAT and I.Q. tests, which, he observed, could be used to discriminate against different races, locking them out of academic and professional opportunities, and for even darker purposes like eugenics.

Ironically, it was Rust who had first invited Kogan to meetings at the Psychometrics Center in 2012. "I thought this was a nice, hospitable thing to do to a new university lecturer," said Rust of the invitation he now regrets.

Although there is a dispute of who the founders of Cambridge Analytica are, it was created for the sole purpose of manipulation. Once Cambridge Analytica was established, it used algorithms and analytics to mark the people who would be most susceptible and open to particular messages based on the topics they researched around 2014. Thus, the *Chosen Ones* were born.

Specific words and phrases were then tested on people from different areas to assess their reactions to phrases like "drain the swamp," "build a wall," and many more. Everything was by design for the *Chosen Ones*.

Trump purposefully targeted the vulnerabilities of his *Chosen Ones* during the 2016 election. "Remember when Jared Kushner, an American investor, real-estate developer, and newspaper publisher who is currently a senior advisor to his father-in-law, Donald Trump, bragged about paying $8 million for tech companies to target voters?

Once Trump announced his campaign, Cambridge Analytica advised him to allocate funds for the areas researchers found most responsive: Michigan, Pennsylvania, and Florida.

Hypnosis, combined with the help of Cambridge Analytica, was enormously helpful to Trump. Thus, we arrived where we are today -- with a President with no moral compass, a narcissistic Peter Pan who never grew up.

Steve Bannon, an alt-right radio host and White House Chief Strategist for the first seven months of Trump's administration, told journalist Michael Lewis in February 2018, "We got elected to drain the swamp, lock her up, build a wall. This was pure anger. Anger and fear is what gets the people rushing to the polls." He added, "The Democrats don't matter. The real opposition is the media. And the way to derail them is to flood the zone with shit."

Flooding the zone with shit continues today, and we are all guilty of contributing. Whether we watch, add to, or ignore the shit, the more it piles up. These days, any news that does not cover Trump's antics is no longer worthy of our attention. We have become accustomed to a level of behavior from the office, and Trump keeps us captivated each time he ups the ante, although now it even appears nonsensical, erratic, and at times, plain mad. His recent misuse of hypnotic techniques and outlandish statements causes me to wonder if he fired his coach.

Ephrat Levni, a writer for *Quartz* magazine and a lawyer, wrote that although Cambridge Analytica has claimed bankruptcy and was dismantled, her research shows that a new company was incorporated in

TRUMP CAN WIN IN 2020

Nevada in February 2018 by Andrew Van Noy, CEO of Cloud Commerce. It just so happens that Cloud Commerce bought out the media marketing company for Trump's 2020 election campaign.

On June 15, 2018, the Associated Press reported that the staffers from Cambridge Analytica are now with a new company named Data Propria. As their name implies, Data Propria is preoccupied with data collection to target voters and consumers. Guess who is employed with Data Propria as well? David Wilkinson, Cambridge Analytica's lead data scientist, and others formerly employed by Cambridge Analytica. I highly recommend you pay attention and do your own research. Please do not take my word or anyone's word for that matter. Stay informed!

We are all well aware of the data research that boosted Trump's campaign, but hypnosis techniques certainly helped push him to the finishing line.

To outline some of the techniques Trump uses, I will begin with Anchoring.

You may be familiar with Ivan Pavlov's classical conditioning of dogs. In short, Pavlov observed that his dogs salivated whenever their food was served. He began ringing a bell anytime he served the dogs' food, linking food with the bell in the dogs' brains. Eventually, ringing the bell alone was enough to get the dogs to salivate, whether there was food present or not.

Anchoring is the same idea. If you were to play a loud "BEEP" right before throwing an object at your friend's head multiple times, their subconscious would associate that "BEEP" with getting hit on the head and would instill fear within them. Eventually, if you play the noise, you'll find your friend bracing for impact even if your hands are empty.

TRUMP CAN WIN IN 2020

An example of an anchor is when Trump walks out on stage, patriotic music that we associate with pride and joy plays in the background. The feelings of pride and joy are then associated with Trump. This is called transference. Each time that music is played, the same response is elicited in the voter.

Trump also uses trigger words to evoke fear, and he consistently repeats them in his dialogue. One most recent trigger word he was "treason." Another is "revolt." These send alarm bells through our nation.

I would venture to say that the White House staff is also being coached. This is what our teacher Thomas, encourages for the sake of compliance. If you *Google* Trump, Pence, and Pelosi during a White House meeting, you will see that Pence appears to be in a constant trance.

Another technique I have noticed that Trump frequently uses is shock value and confusion, which deliberately distracts the conscious mind.

You must ask yourself:

1. Is coal really coming back?

2. Did he really cut taxes for the middle class?

3. Did I really think he would build a wall after his name's sake to keep people he fears out of the country?

If you answered yes to any of these questions, I highly recommend you go back to the drawing board and do more research into Trump.

One valuable source of factual information is the second volume of the Mueller Report. When it was released, Trump was quoted as saying, "Oh no, this is the end of my presidency, I'm f*cked," as cited by Jeff Sessions.

To make the report more readily available and understood, Hollywood actors created a comedic reading of it. This report highlights the fact that Trump wants you to remain in the dark and in a trance, like many Americans who prefer to be spoon-fed narratives, whether they be true or false.

I highly recommend you dig deeper if you are brave and willing to face the truth. I urge you to read the Mueller report for yourself. Mueller's live testimony, in my opinion, did not do justice to the magnitude of the deception that took place at camp Trump. At the very least, read a breakdown of the report. Several books are breaking down the report for readers to understand.

Long before Trump announced his intentions to run for election in 2016, the data collected by Cambridge

Analytica showed that the people living in the Rust Belt would respond to talk and fears of immigration and foreign invasion by migrant workers, and he purposefully seized on those worries.

Remember that these tests began before his decision to run, as stated earlier, so the people they focused on were mostly blue-collar workers and white men afraid of changes and who dreaded the extinction of their race. There is no more significant horror than the fear of becoming extinct, and Trump gladly seized on those fears, and he also focused on those who felt left behind.

Once these types of workers felt an affinity for the President and that he genuinely cared about them, they would not let that security go so easily. Remember that Trump said that he could shoot someone down and not lose a single fan. His diehard fans are here to stay. Why would they let go of what they think is a real connection? His supporters believe he genuinely cares and is looking out for them and their families. When we train a nation to hate, we promote racism, division, and segmentation.

Think about it. To lose that close connection would be devastating; it would short circuit the voter's brain. It would be gut-wrenching to discover that you have been used. No one wants to hear or believe that the man they cherish was a common manipulator. We would rather go out and kill, which some have in the name of Trump than abandon our core beliefs. Once that connection is embedded deeply into one's psyche, it becomes part of one's identity. This is why I say it comes with great responsibility to enter another person's world,

Another group they believed to be highly suggestible are the Evangelicals. They believed Evangelicals to have "blind faith" literally.

Tim Albert, who wrote *American Carnage*, stated during a CNN interview that Trump said, Those F**king Evangelicals, to his republican lawmakers, while bragging about how he Lured them. One must ask the question, why are they so loyal to Trump? Is it indeed blind faith? Do they believe that Trump truly is a modern-day savior?

Pay attention! None of this was by accident. Instead, it is all by design.

Chapter 7

Questionable Behavior

Trump ran a campaign against immigrants and chain migration. Yet we all know that the people he most often employed were undocumented migrants as revealed by the *New York Times*, and apparently, he went to great lengths to hide that fact. Why wouldn't he employ hard working loyal people who were paid less for their hard labor? I wonder who he thinks is going to clean his Maro-Largo mansion? Is the plan to keep Black and brown people down so that they have to work at his hotels? Nothing he does makes sense to me. I cannot begin to guess his intentions.

Then, there is the subject of chain migration; his wife, Melania, was an immigrant, and her parents recently became citizens through chain migration.

Journalist and author Michael D'Antonio reminded us during a recent CNN interview that Trump's grandfather was an economic migrant. On October 7, 1885, Friedrich Trump, a sixteen-year-old German barber, bought a one-way ticket to America, where he was welcomed with open arms. He eventually made a small fortune in New York, something his grandson should have been proud of, but instead, Trump denied his German roots and claimed that his grandfather descended from Scandinavia (Donald Trump, *The Art of the Deal*). Now Trump has designed a system that would cause economic migrants, just like his grandfather, to die crossing the river across Mexico to America with toddlers under their shirts, all the while blaming Democrats for the crisis, I believe he manufactured.

America was built by migrants seeking economic future.

Trump ran his campaign on the promise of having products made in America, yet his garments and just about anything with the "TRUMP" label are made in other parts of the world. I find that a bit hypocritical. How a man touts one thing and does the exact opposite is beyond me. Yet, that is exactly what I have found in Trump. To me, his words don't match his actions, which concerns me.

Worse yet, was his claim of draining the swamp, while he has been living in the swamp. I think he almost exclusively engages in nepotism and consistently violates the government ethics law (2635.702), which states that public office shall not be used for private gain. He blatantly is enjoying the swamp he was supposed to have drained. Maybe, *LIKE PIGS*, he found too much delicious pleasure in it that he could not bring himself to drain the muck of the swamp; instead, he decided to enjoy it.

Then there is the cloud that persistently lurks over Trump in regard to his relationship with the Kremlin. It is said that Trump desperately sought a relationship with Vladimir Putin for several years. So much so that he maneuvered a meeting only to be disappointed when he got there. Putin being the super-intelligent one and savvy at the art of mind games, sent someone in his place to meet Trump. That only made Trump's desire to be in Putin's good favor and his admiration for the man become even more of a desperate need. Remember this is a man, as alluded to earlier, that desperately needs love and approval and to be seen as powerful. But the Ex KGB being no stranger to psychological games, played on his desperation. He would string Trump along, or as the youngsters would say these days, he placed Trump on the hook.

TRUMP CAN WIN IN 2020

In Luke Harding's book, *Collusion*, Christopher David Steele was quite a reliable source of information having held a senior post at M16's Russian desk in London in 2006. The SIS or M16 is the United Kingdom's foreign intelligence service. Steele was an expert on Russia and was offered the job of uncovering the Kremlin's innermost secrets with relation to Donald Trump. "Its conclusion would shake the American intelligence community and cause a political earthquake not seen since the dark days of President Richard Nixon and Watergate." To say the least, what Steele found was indeed sensational and resulted in the infamous Dossier that would become the source of many sleepless nights for the President-elect. It accused President Trump of "Collusion with a foreign power," the gravest of crimes. According to Luke Harding's in his book.

Easy to believe because of Trump's need to have a relationship with Putin, as stated earlier. That desperation would make Trump a vulnerable target for the razor-sharp mind of Putin, the ex KGB.

Clearly unproven, our new President-designate was under a cloud of suspicion, nonetheless. Trump was the Kremlins' candidate, went the whispers.

Trump's own behavior during the campaign did not help matters, asking Moscow to continue leaking his opponent, Hilary Clintons' email, when it was alleged that the Russia hacked and leaked Hilary's emails to help Trump.

At a Florida Rally on July 4, 2016, Trump said, "Russia if you are listening, I hope you are able to find the thirty thousand emails that are missing. I really think you will be rewarded mightily."

I am sure you are asking, "What did he mean when he said, you will be rewarded mightily?"

Interestingly, Moscow had stolen republican national committee emails but did not publish those. They only publish the ones that would hurt Trump's Rival.

TRUMP CAN WIN IN 2020

The emails were not quite as sensational and scandalous as Trump's personal life. Still, Trump being the marketer and salesman that he is, he seized the opportunity to send home the message "Crooked Hilary," which was already one of the words researched for the Chosen Ones, and he dominated the media. In reality, what he did was to transfer the description of himself and projected it to Hilary. This is a technique he still uses to his benefit. He does that with his current running opponent Joe Biden, accusing him of nepotism and pay to play. Something that Ivanka Trump, his daughter, does now cutting deals with China while being a White House staffer.

Trump uses that same technique to project his failures to act early enough during the early warnings of a pandemic. Instead, he claims that Obama left faulty tests in the stockpile. In actuality, the 2020 Pandemic is a new disease, so Obama could not have left faulty testing equipment or supplies. The truth is that the Obama administration left a step by step "pandemic playbook for dummies" for this administration, which they ignored. Later I can get back to some truths about the pandemic as I traveled to Asia during SARS and Ebola. I am well aware of how those were handled. Then there was the consistent praise on Putin.

Everyone else seems to be on Trump's semi-literate irate rants on Twitter while most were in bed.

This Putin/Trump romance could not be based on chemistry for the two had not met.

Apparently, this was more like infatuation and longing on Trump's part to be in Putin's good grace. This allegiance would continue to date.

This type of behavior by Trump would only help raise the question, had Putin been blackmailing our President? There was no other explanation for Trump's undying infatuation. There were rumors that Trump's finances were in shambles. After all, he never showed his tax returns, he had many bankruptcies, and the joke was that he never pays debts. Although he flamboyantly claimed to be a multi-millionaire.

Was he indebted to the Russians? Is Trump over-leveraged owing an enormous amount of money to banks abroad?

In 2016, Luke Harding and a colleague went to London to meet Steele, now self-employed. Steele, although reserved, offered suggestions. "You need to look at the contracts for hotel and land deals" he said. "Check their values, against monies Trump secured via loans."

Harding believed this was in reference to Trump's former house in Florida, which Trump had bought in 2004 for 41 million and sold four years later to a Russian oligarch for 95 million, potentially leaving him vulnerable to blackmail.

Two days later, Steele's work, which was years in the making, landed on President Obama's desk.

According to Harding, Steele spent twenty-two years as a British intelligence officer, part of that time was in Moscow. In 2009, after a personal tragedy, he began a private practice after setting up Orbis.

So how did Steele come to be commissioned to research Trump and produce the now-famous Dossier?

Around the same time that Steele set up Orbis, Simpson, a journalist, cofounded his own commercial research and political intelligence firm, based in Washington DC called Fusion GPS. Simpson and Steele met in 2009. They knew the same FBI people and had the same expertise in Russia and they began a partnership.

Steele was regarded as the Russian espionage expert and a credible source who had authored hundreds of reports on Russia and Ukraine that was shared within the state department, says Harding, and sent up to Secretary of State John Kerry, between 2014-2016.

During the 2016 presidential primaries, the Washington Beacon, backed by Trump's wealthy opponent, Paul Singer, commissioned Fusion to investigate Trump and Simpson approached Steele. Steele then started to scrutinize Paul Manafort, Trump's new campaign manager.

From April 2016, Steele investigated Trump on behalf of the DNC, Fusion's anonymous client. Paul Singer had lost interest once Trump became the Presumptive nominee, so senior democrats seeking to elect Hilary took over the Contract. The National Democratic Committee became Fusion's new client. Fusion had already approached Steele before the transfer had taken place, so Steele continued his investigation. The obvious question for Steele at the time was, "Are there any business ties to Russia?"

What Steele uncovered was "Hair raising," Steele told friends. Steele had stumbled on a well-advanced conspiracy that involved the Kremlin and Trump.

Steele sources claim that the Russian intelligence had been secretly cultivating Trump for at least five years and that the operation had exceeded beyond Moscow's wildest dreams-it was just possible that Trump might become the next U.S. President.

In June 2016, Steele typed his first memo and sent it to Fusion. The headline read, "U.S. presidential election: Republican candidate Donald Trump's activities in Russia and compromising relationship with the Kremlin."

Sixteen sensational memos in all were sent to Fusion between June 2014-2016. After July 2016, intelligence was scarce after the Trump Russia relationship was under scrutiny. If Steele's Reporting was correct, Trump had been colluding with Russia. Each party gained something from the relationship. Apparently, Trump received information from the

Kremlin via his inner circle. It seemed that Russia's top Spying agencies were investing efforts to get close to Trump and his family and friends, not to mention his campaign manager, now in jail, Paul Manafort.

Steele's memo alleged that Trump had unusual sexual proclivities that would make him an easy target for blackmail. Allegedly that memo offered salacious details including one particular encounter in Russia that included "golden showers (urination)" with prostitutes at the Ritz Carlton Presidential suite where the Obama's would stay. He deliberately viled the bed because he hated the Obamas. This room was known to be under FSB control with bugs and cameras. But the fascinating part of the plots, said Steele sources, was that Trump's associate and Russian spies had a series of secret meetings around Europe. Finally, they alleged that Trump had coordinated with Russia and co-paid for the Clinton email hacks to benefit his political campaign.

The report was marked as a confidential/sensitive source with names of the prominent individuals in bold-**TRUMP**, **PUTIN**, **CLINTON**. The report began with a summary, and supportive details and sources cited generically, "A senior foreign minister" or a "former top intelligence figure."

How sure was Steele of his sources and his reporting? This question was essential as the information was so damning. Steele was adamant about his credibility and the credibility of the report. One associate described him as solid and not likely to report gossip. "If he puts something in a report," said his colleague, "It's because its credible."

On a separate front, the GCHQ, the government communications headquarters, or Uk's eavesdropping agency, carrying out standard "collection" against Moscow's target, found that they were talking to people associated with Trump that formed a suspicious pattern and continued through the first half of 2016. This information was handed to the U.S. as part of routine sharing. The U.S. was slow to show interest in the extensive nature of these contacts between trumps team and Moscow because of laws that prohibit U.S. agencies from examining private communications of U.S. citizens without a warrant.

That summer, the head of GCHQ agency, Robert Hunnigan, flew to the USA to personally brief the CIA. The matter was so important that it was handled at the directors' level face to face. Later the director would only confirm "it's sensitive."

Meanwhile, the FBI received information from Steele. Steele realized that the information was "A radioactive hot potato." The FBI continued to move cautiously, as it could not intervene or go public with material involving a presidential candidate. Steele Frustration continued to grow, and Simpson decided to take another route. They reached out to news magazines, and David Corn from *Mother Jones* wrote about the Dossier on October 31. Democratic senators grew exasperated. The FBI seemed keen on trashing Hilary's reputation while sitting on explosive material concerning Trump. Harry Reed, then republican minority leader, wrote to James Comey, "The Public has a right to know this information." The frantic information came to nothing, and Trump won the election.

By November, the Dossier reached the top officers of the Obama administration, but it was too late.

Chapter 8

Path of Least Resistance

People are moved by fear, and for Trump, that was the path of least resistance. One way Trump was able to get into the minds of his subjects was by preying on their fears. Using fear, he vividly described foreign invasions by migrant workers in caravans climbing up walls. He used words that would evoke fear and terror in his followers.

Repetition is another hypnosis strategy that Trump often uses. Once again, the people that Cambridge

Analytica researched showed that White men would react to the fear of becoming extinct or becoming a minority race. Trump used the research to exacerbate those fears.

To bypass the critical factor, I have observed that Trump distracts the conscious mind in many ways by first connecting to his subjects with laughter, then by using repetition to instill into the unconscious what he wants them to hear. While the conscious mind is distracted, he embeds his commands into the subconscious.

Another technique he uses is anchoring by using music at his rallies. Usually, he uses the same music while walking onto the stage to fire off the feel-good anchors. His subjects have become anchored to the red "Make America Great Again" MAGA hat, evoking emotions and implying he would be the hero that would bring "America" back to greatness.

He often uses the technique of social proof. This is done through vague generalizations such as when he says, "Many people said so, so it must be true." One interesting way I have seen him use this technique is by citing Obama, particularly when he wants to connect with Obama's followers. Obama was extremely popular, so Trump naturally uses Obama as social proof through lines such as, "Obama said this or did that, so it must be true," or "Obama wanted a wall" so a wall must be good for America, even though Obama did not say that.

Social proof is used to connect oneself to another person, object or subject that is socially well-regarded. It is often vague when Trump uses it. For example, "Many people said so," "They all say I am great," or "I'm smart because they all say I am."

Have you ever heard him say, "We are the smartest, and they know we are smart" or something to that effect? He is basically telling his subjects they are smart because they are with him, without stating it directly. He says it over and over again to drill the positive reinforcement and feel-good anchors into his followers. Obviously, the effect is not easy to verify, but who would disagree when told they are smart? We must pay close attention to how we are manipulated. Even I, admittedly, have admired the man at times, and I have studied this communication art for twenty years.

These techniques are powerful tools that must not be given to the unethical.

One example of a group that used this tool that was meant to be used as "a force for good" for their own narcissistic gain was NXIVM, an American multi-level marketing company. NXIVM was a self-empowerment group turned Cult led by Keith Raniere and Nancy Zulsman.

Nancy Zulsman was a nurse practitioner who mastered Ericksonian Hypnosis and NLP around the late 80s. She studied with some of the greatest teachers but ended up with Keith Rainere, a great manipulator who ended up in prison after NXIVM was investigated. The case is in public records. Once again, I personally believe that powerful tools should never be given to the unethical.

Chapter 9

Continuing Down This Road

If we continue down this road, we will hand the election of 2020 to the Donald on a silver platter. According to a *Politico* news article written by Charles Sykes on June 25, 2019, Democrats could blow it and hand victory over to the Trump 2020 campaign, even though "Donald Trump is historically unpopular because the last three years have cemented his public image as a profoundly dishonest, erratic, narcissistic, twitter-addicted bully. As a result, 57% of voters have said they would not vote to reelect him. The article continues with eleven pointers.

Trump has an unfair advantage that his "raving fans" cannot even see because they are too deep in trance, much like the followers of NXIVM, self-empowerment group-turned cult.

It's also hard to keep up with Trump because he is purposefully all over the place, like a boxer that cannot be reached in a boxing ring. He frequently returns to his subjects to fire off the "anchors" and keep them in a state of trance. Honestly, I believe some are willing to kill for him. He vocalizes these violent trigger sentences at rallies. Some new trigger words he throws out are "third term" and "revolt."

I believe anyone who wants to unseat him must study his techniques to inoculate himself/ herself against them. These techniques were never intended for egotistical use or needs. They were intended to be used as a "force for good." Thus, I still believe these tools should be taught with discernment in mind.

I can't go into the details because I would be announcing my suggestions to him and his base, at this point, which is for me to know and you to find out. Actually, I don't know it all, but much like the athletes, contenders must prepare their offense. Not so much defense, because once he "got ya" it's too late.

I would suggest at that point to make it a part of your debate strategy and move on to another topic. Don't let it stick. Just let it slide right off you, and no one will notice. I can also say we all know what gets under his skin; and I'll leave it at that as that is already saying a bit too much. Just keep him preoccupied and off the media circuit.

He is already vexed with his *Fox News* "bromances" because they allowed Democratic town halls. I think it would be best to keep him busy and derailed, and that is easy to do.

Allow me to demonstrate how I would handle a distraction or failed situation if I were doing a group trance/hypnosis, and someone walks in late or coughs. I would include it in your trance induction or your speech.

Don't let anyone see you sweat. Comedians do this very well. I would say, "As you notice the noise in the room, or door closing, just allow that to take you even deeper, *thaaat's* right."

It's not wise to pretend something is not going on; it only throws you off your game. Trump is the only one who can pretend something that blatantly happened, did not happen, and he honestly believes that the cult followers would believe his lies.

I have faith in my fellow humans, and I believe sooner than later, he will do himself in. We cannot be as stupid as he thinks we are. NO WAY!

I believe we were given the ability to think and discern, unlike the lower-level animals that he thinks we are. I must believe in my fellow human's ability to think for ourselves.

One example of a missed opportunity was when Trump walked around Hilary, in her space, during their debate. I believe he masterminded this dance to throw her off and intimidate her. She could have inoculated herself and the audience by simply saying, "Dude, I see you. Ain't working" or "Getting in my space makes you a loser" -- in a joking manner, of course.

Laughter is always the go-to "pattern interrupt" or anything to make the audience notice and crack up and throw him off. He is natural with his facial expressions that demonstrate to the audience, "What my opponent just said is ridiculous," keeping attention off the topic at hand.

It's not attractive for a woman to model that behavior but find another way to keep the audience's eyes off him and on you. Drown him out somehow with laughter or clapping, anything to distract him, especially if it's unexpected.

TRUMP CAN WIN IN 2020

Remember, his attention span is short. I can't announce too many ways for the candidates to grab hold of this information without the opponent grabbing it first.

Steele's information was out there about the Russians, but the government was way too slow to act, and by the time they decided to move on it, Trump had already won. Please don't be reluctant to prepare for his antics.

All I can say is to study the man and his debate like a football team that will study their opponents. Think of this election as a football game with consequences. Imagine, one hundred years of this new normal -- people hating each other and lawlessness prevailing. Your descendants have no education or means of sustaining themselves. A planet of dictators! Is that what you want? That is if we have a planet left at all.

That would be my advice to the contenders. Anyone who tries to be Trump will fail at it. Michale

Avennati came closest in terms of toughness, but how far did that get him?

Just find your individual way to inoculate yourself against his antics and get ahead of his game. We all know what rattles Trump already. That's a great start. Keep him rattled and keep him preoccupied. Maybe his fan base is never going to come out of a trance but focus on the main population. Attack him where it hurts -- Ivanka. Then again, to a narcissist, no one or nothing matters but himself/herself. Everything else, family included, is a tool for their use.

I am not suggesting that any candidate should target offspring. No decent President would do that. Then again, nothing is in the normal range right now.

What I am saying is to keep Ivanka busy. She works for the people. She has children, and I hope she has some preoccupation with them. She works for the American people and should be held accountable. Scrutinize her every move. Just keep them all exhausted answering tweets because we know he can't stop tweeting. Keep him up at night, tweeting. I would suggest that we give him things to tweet about late in the evening or at night. Study when he responds best to the news. Using algorithms, we can quickly figure out these patterns. Anyway, as I said before, I don't want to give the secrets away. You must be one step ahead of him, and because you already know how easy it is to derail him, I suggest to 2020 contenders get busy.

Remember what Howard Stern said? "He never wanted to be President; it was a publicity stunt." They were friends. He also said that he wished Trump would seek therapy. This is the very reason I have some level of empathy for the man. I don't hate the man himself, but I hate what he has done to the highest office of the most powerful land.

CNN's Don Lemon said something that resonated with me after Trump's 2020 campaign launch. "The cult-like trance starts small."

I believe Lemon is right. Verifiable facts clothed around the command you intend to install. Lemon continues to challenge Cuomo, "Ask any family member of Jim Jones." Jones took them to Guyana. It started with aligning with their value of Christianity. Little by little, he got them to the point where he could convince them all to commit suicide.

Even more damaging is that Russia probably has more sophisticated plans to infiltrate our system. As I stated earlier, Cambridge Analytica is already in place under the name data *propia*, since its downfall, many of the same people have been preparing for 2020.

We all witnessed Trump's 2020 launch with a venue filled with 20,000 raving fans. This is a phenomenon, and it started with the feel-good music anchored to him as he and Melania walked onto the stage. Music is one of the best anchors because of beats in Hertz. They are favorable to the brain's frequency. Listen to an old song and see how fast it takes you down memory lane.

The sense of smell is another great anchor that real estate agents and department stores use, such as the smell of baked cookies in the home they hope you will buy.

Shortly after his favorite thing to do, which is a rally with his raving fans in a permanent trance, came the hard job -- conflict with Iran. On June 20, 2019, Trump ordered a military strike on Iran only to withdraw with ten minutes left on the clock. Although he claims that the casualty would be too high and all of a sudden he had a Gestalt of awareness and conscience for human lives, but according to what I read on the *New Yorker* by Ben Taub on June 27, 2019, a *Fox News* host, Tucker Carlson had told Trump that a more significant casualty would bar his re-election.

Remember, some of Trump's closest advisors are on *Fox News;* in fact, they frequently have visits and phone chats.

On June 25, 2019, in response to Iran's President, Hassan Rouhani, saying that the White House was "Afflicted by mental retardation," Trump threatened the "obliteration" of Iran. All this is in the article by Ben, but we remember the 2018 tweets in which he said to "Never ever threaten the U.S. again, or you will suffer consequences, the likes of which throughout history have never been suffered before. We are no longer a country that would stand for your demented words of violence and death."

"Be cautious," Trump warned in a July 2018 tweet. It was written in capital letters.

Iran, like the rest of the world, is laughing at Trump, his White House, and America, jeering that our White House suffers from dementia and mental retardation, among other demeaning smears.

TRUMP CAN WIN IN 2020

Worse, Iran shot down our drones. That was a blatant provocation. Iran won that one, and the joke was on us.

That being said, we are glad another potential world war was avoided. This was a decision Congress should have made, instead of the advisors at FOX with our country's future in their hands.

The North Korean Dictator, Kim Jong-un, calls our bluff and jeers us continuously, calling it bravado and jibberish on Twitter.

Trump, of course, spins the narrative and makes himself to be a hero that saved the day and avoided casualties.

In reality, this behavior is insane to me. Who gets briefed ten minutes before a possible world-changing catastrophe? We no longer have allies, so who would go to combat with us? We are only about Americans, so we pull out of the peace agreement by ourselves.

Chapter 10

Our Fear of Becoming the Minority Race

White Anglo-Saxons becoming the minority is a fear tactic, and I believe that Trump uses it for his benefit. Demographers long predicted this notion, and it has created a great deal of fear and anxiety.

Wisely, big companies such as Procter & Gamble have become more inclusive over the years. They have begun to prepare because they knew the demographics of non-whites would comprise the bulk of the consumers. Not only have they announced the change of major logos, but they have also started to hire more minorities in marketing and provided scholarships to prepare for the future. In other words, they have embraced the change that is to come rather than to fight it. Change will happen, no matter how much we resist.

Thus here rests the biggest fear of all consciousness -- the fear of extinction. Even a cancer cell competes for survival. Fear of extinction was also used by Adolf Hitler to instill fear. His plan to fight change did not work out too well for him. Apparently, it was anthropologist Friedrich Blumenbach around 1700-1800 who decided that people from the Causcus Mountains in Georgia most resembled his race. Blumenbach did not put these races he coined into hierarchies. Historians believed that in his work *De generis humani varietate nativa,* 1795, he rejected hierarchy and instead emphasized unity. The discrimination along racial lines came later and from other men. It is believed that the Caucus region came to be due to the tectonic plate shifts. More recent theories suggest that Albinos, common in Africa, migrated to the Causcus mountains to escape persecution as it was believed to be a curse to lack melanin, when in fact, it's a genetic defect. They began to migrate northward through Egypt. These theorists believe that was how the Caucus race began.

We, as humans, must be willing to adapt to change. The original man was from Africa, but as man moved to lands further away, man lost the great melanin. It is believed that early migration began over two million years ago with *homo erectus* "out of African migration." Yes, the narratives of human evolution are often contentious. DNA evidence shows, according to *Wikipedia*, that human evolution should not be seen as a simple linear or branched progression, but as a mix of related species. As much as we would rather conveniently believe that science is a big liar, it's becoming increasingly difficult to deny that we are all related.

So let's just suppose for the sake of humor that science does exist. Why so much fear? Is it that we, as we became lighter and lighter, became frailer? Is that it? Are we that afraid and fragile? We must ask, is it that deep down we harbor the belief that we are still defective, evil Albinos who will be persecuted for lacking the great melanin, so we persecute those with it before they persecute us? We must ponder these things. Or, is it that deep down we committed evil acts against the Native Americans and Blacks -- our human cousins?

Why the fear? The smart companies such as Proctor and Gamble did not put a plan in place to keep brown people down. Instead, they innovated. They knew they needed to train our brown cousins and send them all over the world to manage and study cultures. That is called innovation and smarts, not fear.

Even Uber has a super-smart lady friend of the family who goes all over the world studying diverse cultures so that they can become smart at innovating.

Let's face the facts here, people of all colors are on this planet, and sooner or later we must cohesively live side by side with our cousins whom we may feel are inferior to us. There is no other way. We cannot stop growth and evolution. Let's suppose the melanated people were still persecuting white-skinned people, fearing they were evil. How would that feel? We must ponder this too.

Yes again, I know that many deny evolution, but I have always questioned things even while the preacher stood at the pulpit, telling us we were wretched souls destined to die in Hell's fire.

I could not bring myself to believe that. *God did not make me that way*, I thought. So very conflicted as a teen, I would go up during the healing time for the wretched sinners, and I would cry my eyes out. That blessed, caring pastor felt for me, and as he put his hand on my head and prayed, I would cry even more. It was not at all because my wretchedness was being healed. It was because I felt conflicted and sad about my conflicts. I just needed to study and learn for myself. Every chance I had, I would sneak to some seminar.

I wanted answers. I remember when I was twenty-one, I met the founder of Aveda, Horst Rechelbacher. He introduced me to his swami. Off I went to some jungle on the east coast. I was picked up and driven two hours to the ashram. That early morning, I met Swami Rama, if I am not mistaken on the name. He gave me a mantra that I don't even remember now.

Life was horrendously painful as a teen, and I was painfully shy. I remember as far back as when I was a preteen, and I was bullied for being scrawny. The pain was so unbearable I locked myself in the one bathroom we had at the time and curled up into a fetal position crying until no tears were left. I believe the dreams I had of becoming a mafia boss or beating my bullies into a pulp did not subside until years later after I learned about self-help techniques.

Luckily, I had a mind that needed logic and knowledge, which might have saved me from becoming a deathly sick person in this world. I eventually stopped going to church and set out on my own to search for answers. Nowadays, I look back on those painful times as blessings. Were it not for those pressing questions, I might not have become who I am today.

I came to America at the age of fourteen and found the education here a bit lacking because I always had answers to the questions they asked at school. I didn't raise my hand because I had an accent.

Eventually, my teachers would call on me to tell the answer in class. That made me feel good about myself. I remember one teacher trying to shame me when I studied at a Catholic school because I had been busy daydreaming of a land far away where the streets were made of gold. This land was called

America. However, back then, there were no such things as calculators. She had a long math formula on the blackboard, and she called on me to solve the problem. I did, much to her surprise. Inside, I secretly felt that I had "showed her up."

I now summon these memories to anchor myself when I am feeling unsure. I pick a specific touch to fire off that anchor when needed. Since I may need these anchors most in public, I touch my middle finger to my thumb to fire off the anchor or something to that effect.

Chapter 11

Trump's Undying Love Affair with Dictators

Have you ever even asked yourself the question, why? More importantly, what does Trump have to hide? I wonder why those in a trance never ask questions. I come from a family of diehard Republicans, but my family immediately noticed the abnormalcy and changed. Some candidates nominated themselves during the 2016 election. I believe this was a vote for Trump.

His narcissism was obvious to me, and possibly even to the untrained eye. Yet, no one from his base asked the question? I am certain many Republicans in the

White House saw it, but they quickly fell in line rather than succumbing to his wrath. They would rather have sold their souls to the Devil for a quarter of a dollar.

One technique that is frequently used by his friend, Thomas, is a punishment technique. I still don't think anyone caught on. It took me years. I won't say what it is called because thousands will know who this teacher is. Once again, I owe a lot to him. It's basically a form of ridicule on stage if the participant did not get the right answer. It's all done, I suppose, for the good, but it's painful to watch, and some come away feeling more pain. I know some who came away feeling like failures. Knowing what I now know, I believe the technique is to achieve compliance.

Perhaps you may have seen the TED Talk experiment by Frans de Waal about moral behavior in animals. In the experiment, two monkeys are paid unequally, and the monkey that was not treated fairly protested. It was sad to watch the monkey feel it was being treated unfairly.

Pavlov used dogs and anchored them to get them to salivate. We train animals this way, and it is the same way with humans and rewards or punishment. That's what Trump does to people who don't "behave." They face ridicule and fall in line, one by one. They are beaten down.

Thomas' seminars we attended were often held for seventeen hours or more. Again, when exhausted, it is easier to bypass the critical factor. People achieved the results they seek. Likewise, Trump achieves compliance from his staff using punishment along with his charm to get them under his spell.

I am not here to argue for one side or negate the other. I believe that Trump's subjects should have a chance to choose and not follow him around like sheep. Yes, we do have a good economy, but his base is not reaping the benefits of this booming economy.

TRUMP CAN WIN IN 2020

His base is suffering. The economy was on the upswing from the previous administration. The economy is cyclical. However, if you don't read, you would not know that, would you?

Social proof is a big factor when using these techniques, and few brave souls would violate social proof. Who wants to be ridiculed for asking a dumb question? That's what Trump would say if he did not agree and, worse, you would get axed for "bringing bad news to the King."

What did Kim Jong-un do to his people when he did not get an agreement at the meeting with his loving fan Trump? It is believed that they were killed because the meeting was a failure. Kim was embarrassed.

The reason optics are so crucial to Trump is that of social proof. "I had the biggest audience at the inauguration."

Michael Brackman

On the very rare occasion, I held a very small class with my friend Claudio, I picked the smallest room for the training, and I positioned the chairs close together in a semicircle. I also used a higher chair than those in the audience for the optics. I don't often allow others to know that side of my world, and I believe that it is because that shy person is still inside. The few times I have allowed others to know that I have been studying this technology for close to twenty years, not to mention my queries from Buddhist monks, my shamanistic journeys, my queries at the Egyptian Pyramids, I have been pretty successful using these tenets; however, my greatest success is my children.

I have known all my life that if I did not break the cycle of pain, it would continue for a long time, generations, perhaps. I didn't want to leave it to chance, so I went out to change myself.

Howard Stern said in a CNN interview, which I mentioned before, that he doubted Trump would ever seek psychological help. Narcissists can't see anything wrong in or about themselves.

I knew that I had to pave the way for my children, so I tried to help myself. I know their lives are and will be even more splendid than mine. If that is all I accomplish during this lifetime, I will leave this world a satisfied man. Even more, if I can impress upon my fellow human brethren that brown people won't chase White people back to Europe, I will go to my grave happy. We are all from Africa.

Most importantly, we live on this planet called Earth. So, don't worry! We will all be fine as long as we keep the crazy folks away from the red button!

Trump knows that the brown migrants are doing the work the average American will not do, and they are doing it for smaller wages. He depended on them to clean his hotel rooms.

My mother came to America because she was an educational snob and wanted a good education for us that she could not afford. I worked from the age of fourteen at the Eagle Army Navy Store, and my sibling worked from the age of twelve washing dishes.

If all the hardworking consumers left, who would clean his hotel rooms and buy his shirts made in China? I only want people to open their eyes and try to think for themselves.

I'm simply pointing out how ridiculous the idea of a single race seems to be. If that were so, plastic surgeons would not exist or have any work. All the Kardashians have the butts and lips of brown people, and there would be no need either for tanning booths. It seems all of us want a little melanin for ourselves. Could that be the reason for all the fear?

Take the late Nipsey Hussle, though I never heard his name before his early demise. His father is from Eritrea, and he and his brothers were entrepreneurs since they were young boys selling C.D.s outside their house in Los Angeles. By the time of his death, he had purchased much in the Crenshaw neighborhood in Los Angeles. He also had big plans for brown people, reinvesting and reinventing their communities.

Or take Prince, whom I met on Hennnepen Avenue in Minneapolis when we were all young. He came to change the way the music industry conducted business. Prince and Hussle were both extraordinarily productive and successful brown people, yet we are afraid of brown people and of change.

Not a single one of these music icons was fed with a silver spoon. They created their greatness with sweat and blood. It saddens me that I could not appreciate their vision when they were alive, but I do believe thought forms are consciousness, so my brown skin brethren now know how much I regret not showing them love. I only hope we too, will all leave behind positive thought forms.

I hope history will not say we self-destructed. And as far as reparations go, Don Lemon touched on it, and Mitch McConnell made a silly, ignorant statement that none of those "Evildoers," meaning slave owners, is alive today.

Well, why don't we give up some of our wealth then? I would be willing to start a non-profit to help right the wrong. I don't see Trump or McConnell offering up their goods that were achieved through the backbreaking work of slaves or offering to give Indians back their land. Don't pretend that it's over.

Furthermore, remember the Capuchin monkey experiment by Mr. Waal, mentioned just a few paragraphs ago? Unfairness greatly harms the psyche and DNA of generations to come. I much appreciate my ability to see my evil ways as I am far from perfect and often work to self-correct. Personal change requires a willingness to work. If I had never experienced pain, I might not have been motivated to do the work.

Chapter 12

Pay Attention (Or Less of It)

Giving our undivided attention to what we do want is perhaps the best advice I can give anyone who desires to unseat Trump. We all must give him less attention. The whole world has given him their undivided attention, thus creating more of what we don't want.

We certainly do not want a world filled with divisiveness, hate, or anger. Yet, that is exactly what we have chosen, perhaps not consciously, but by default to govern us.

Michael Brackman

Trump won not only by harvesting data about and manipulating our minds, but also captivating our attention. I have come to that realization slowly, and even so, it is not easy to distract myself from the circus. He makes sure there is always pandemonium to garner our attention through the media.

I know that this is a conundrum. Although the news media may know that they are contributing to the phenomena of Trump, they would not exist without viewers. So, we have all, in essence, contributed. We follow the news we want to watch, and news stations compete for our viewership. They know as well as I that we have contributed to the spreading of Trump's propaganda. I wonder if Trump purposefully planned to stage the strike on Iran to create chaos and be front and center of the news only to pull out. He has proudly admitted that he likes chaos.

I pondered that question almost immediately after he called the strike off. What we all need to consider is that the more space we give him in our precious mind, the more of that we create. In other words, we get what we focus on. The demons we see raising their ugly heads were there lying dormant all along and needed to come to the surface. Trump only permitted it to raise its head. Now it's smack dead front-and-center so that we can see it plain as day, but we ought to be careful that it does not control whom we become.

If we continue to be in anger and rage, we continue to stay in fight mode with that energy, and we give it more power.

Many may laugh at Democratic contender Marianne Williamson, but I can see where she was trying to go during the first Democratic debate. It's not a laughing matter. Talking directly to Trump, she said, "You know exactly what you are doing," referring to the hate he spews.

Some may find these ideas funny, but it doesn't matter. What matters is bringing to light the fact that we were and are being manipulated. Maybe

Williamson knows she won't win because many find her teachings to be "Hocus Pocus," but I think it's vital for her to bring awareness to others the way I am through my words. It's somewhat therapy for me because I feel helpless watching people being manipulated so blatantly, yet with no one seeming to notice.

I am not suggesting we bury our heads in the sand or ignore what is taking place. I believe we can take our power back while still maintaining awareness. Realizing that life is full of the unwanted and that we can handle the unwanted as we go along, we remember who we really are -- powerful and worthy human beings. We can do something, and that is exercise our right to vote.

Most importantly, focus on what you want. While it may be hard to dig yourself away from rage, start to think of what you want, slowly. If you feel too far removed or too invested in the doom and gloom, take long walks with your dog, swim, and laugh; do something, anything, that brings you relief. If we can all come to realize together that we can empower ourselves and then begin practicing that, things will change.

Laughter is one quick way to interrupt the downward cycling pattern. Listen to a Deepak Chopra lecture or watch Oprah's *YouTube* videos about self-empowerment, for example. Find something that works for you. Remind yourself that the luminous intent behind all of Trump's antics is to be loved, liked, or approved. He does not mean to be an ugly individual, but as Howard Stern suggested on that interview with Anderson Cooper, he needs therapy, and he had a difficult childhood.

When I allow myself to feel compassion, I experience less anger. Most people stop watching television; however, if the rage is still part of the collective consciousness, then we make no movement toward what we do want. I allow myself to feel sorrow for Trump sometimes because he desperately needs approval.

While we allow ourselves some relief from what we don't want, we must move our thoughts, energy, meditation, prayer, appreciation -- whatever it is you do to make positive movements -- do that slowly on an individual level, and we will find ourselves less interested in him and more interested in what we do want.

While we accomplish that, we must remain focused on what we do want -- a President who has empathy and kindness for all, a leader that is a wise adult.

The bar is so low for what we expect from this President that we easily move on from all his foibles. We must remember that we want a President of strong moral fiber.

Just as actors have found a good way to present the Mueller Report by using comedic readings, we too must find ways to educate without lowering the resonance. We must resonate at a higher frequency of energy to attract that which is likened to us.

The law of resonance says that when two vibrate at different frequencies, they cannot remain the same. One must lower their vibration or raise their frequency to resonate with the other, or at a minimum meet in the middle. The only option I like in this scenario is for us all to raise our frequency.

We cannot continue on the same path, or future generations will live in a whole different kind of world -- one with less goodness until we reach a shallow consciousness. The thought of evolving back into lower consciousness is a very gloomy idea. As a species, we must not go backward.

I had a conversation with my daughter today about this very topic, but I could not find the right words. Teaching someone to reach higher is not easy, and words teach very little.

In NLP, we are thought that only 7% of communication is received through words. So words are hardly an adequate means to express that which I am trying to convey. My daughter finds herself afraid of being cheated on because she had an awful experience as a teenager in love. I did not think that my words helped her much; so, I had to see good experiences in her future for her. I could not help her to find relief from her angst about relationships. So I did it for her. She was too close to the subject. She was already in angst.

A good way is to put a different frame around the subject. In NLP it is called reframing. In her case, she might want to give herself some wiggle room and see it as an experience that made her wiser while it did not kill her. In time, she may find that it made her stronger. For now, the close-up is too raw.

To experience a cinema better, you don't want to be in the first row. It might create some discomfort to be up close to the cinema screen. A little distance gives a better perspective. Because she already has someone who likes her madly, and vice versa, the angst is intensified. So, she may have to go easy with herself and soothe her angst when she is already in a good place and build from there.

I heard Oprah say on one of her *YouTube* videos that a thought lasts seventeen seconds before it's off with momentum. So in her case, she ought to find the good feelings before she is already in angst and stack other good feelings and experiences on to them before the seventeen seconds are up.

I have heard Dr. Richard Bandler, one of the NLP founders, speak about stacking feelings to make changes. He has done this while clients are in hypnotic trances, where he takes them back to times, they were experiencing the unwanted to garner the strong compulsion to make a change. This is a very effective technique.

In the case of Trump, we may want to stack good feelings before going into the lion's den. If I were a news reporter, that would be a helpful technique to use before going into the day to cover Trump. There are many ways to disengage from the current President with a weak moral fiber.

Epilogue

Please, 2020 contenders, make no mistakes. If you want to be a winner, like Trump, you'll have to pay close attention to what he does. Study him like I have and learn from him. No, devour those valuable techniques. However, remain aware of them so you can inoculate yourself from them.

The simplest technique is mirroring (pace, pace - PACE, LEAD) to establish rapport and connection.

Mirroring and pacing set up the environment for success. The subject begins to feel understood and cared about. The walls begin to crumble.

Modeling and anchoring are other essential techniques. Embed your messages between your verifiable "yes" statements over and over. Make that your number one practice.

An anchor could be a space that you mark out for your good messages and another for what is "bad."

An anchor could be a word that produces laughter, and you can mark it out each time with a gesture so that whenever you want those good laughing chemicals to be released, repeat the gesture so that the audience can also return to that good feeling.

The quickest way to bypass the critical factor is laughter. Again, laughing releases good chemical feelings.

Pay attention to your subjects; know them and learn to work large audiences. Make them your undying, raving fans.

All that being said, the techniques do not deliver the results that a President needs to deliver.

Trump keeps having to go back to his raving fans to fire off the anchors and re-establish his place in their hearts because at least sixty percent of America was not suggestible. However, admittedly, he keeps the attention on him either by shock value or distractions.

The reason that only 40% was hypnotized, I believe, is that for one, he chose a specific group that was most susceptible to hypnotic suggestions. At least, they were easily identifiable.

Have you ever wondered how a stage hypnotist can put people in a trance very quickly? The quickest I have ever seen anyone do this was Paul McKenna in London. They give verifiable instructions and watch the reactions. In my case, I was in the front row and could not stop laughing. I was on the floor in tears.

The verifiable statements went something like this, "As you sit on your chair, notice the feel of the chair on your buttocks."

He followed at a fast pace and with a few more verifiable suggestions. It was that quick, and that easy.

ABOUT THE AUTHOR

Trump May Win 2020 is Michael Brackman's debut book. Michael Brackman has been an avid student of psychology, sociology, and subjects concerning human behavior and potential since the age of 15. He has a keen passion for quantum physics and sees humans as a microcosm of the macrocosm. As an adult, he continued to study the human condition with shamans and yogis in hopes of finding answers to the questions that lingered in his mind. Later, in his adult years, that he met his teacher, Thomas.

While studying with Thomas, Michael learned that one effective and quick method to alter behaviors or habits is using the tools hypnosis and neurolinguistic programming. He positioned himself to learn from many great masters in the field including Thomas himself.

Thomas' first workshop changed the trajectory of Michael's life. He returned for many years to work with Thomas to help others in the process of overcoming negative lifelong habits. To this day Michael feels great love and sense of loyalty to Thomas and his team.

Michael then went on to obtain a Master's certification in Ericksonian Hypnosis and Neurolinguistic Programming. Michael's passion was born of a deep desire to change himself and erase past pain. It is often said, "Out of the pain comes the muse!"

TRUMP CAN WIN IN 2020

Michael Brackman has been writing for decades. He is physically active, loves family time, traveling around the world, and has a deep passion for karate.

Michael Brackman

STUDY NOTES

TRUMP CAN WIN IN 2020

STUDY NOTES

Michael Brackman

STUDY NOTES

TRUMP CAN WIN IN 2020

STUDY NOTES

Michael Brackman

STUDY NOTES

TRUMP CAN WIN IN 2020

STUDY NOTES

Michael Brackman

STUDY NOTES

TRUMP CAN WIN IN 2020

STUDY NOTES

Michael Brackman

STUDY NOTES

TRUMP CAN WIN IN 2020

STUDY NOTES

Michael Brackman

STUDY NOTES

Glossary

For more information on these terms, follow the attached links.

Anchoring: The process of associating an internal response with an internal or external trigger. It is similar to the conditioning technique used by Pavlov.

http://www.nlpu.com/Articles/artic28.htm
https://inlpcenter.org/nlp-anchoring/

Critical Factor: The part of the human mind that accepts or rejects information and decides whether that information will be allowed into the subconscious mind based on whether this information is compatible with existing beliefs, values, and ways of thinking.

Michael Brackman

http://EzineArticles.com/3229793

https://thrivingaudios.com/your-critical- factor-manipulation-and-hypnosis/

Embedded Command: An NLP technique for planting a thought beneath another
person's conscious awareness.

http://attitudeadjustment.tripod.com/Books/Persuade.htm

https://plaintifftriallawyertips.com/the-psychology-of-embedded-commands

Modeling: A technique through which one creates models based on others' expertise for the purposes of learning and teaching new skills.

https://inlpcenter.org/what-is-neuro- linguistic-programming-nlp/

Neuro Linguistic Programming: A set of skills for understanding and using nonverbal communication.

https://inlpcenter.org/what-is-neuro- linguistic-programming-nlp/

https://www.instructionalsolutions.com/blog/nominalizations-in-writing

https://www.nlpworld.co.uk/nlp-glossary/n/nominalization/

Pattern Interrupt: Interrupting a pattern of behavior or thoughts to induce a trance or interrupt an unresourceful pattern of behavior.

https://excellenceassured.com/nlp-training/nlp-certification/pattern-interrupt

https://nlp-mentor.com/pattern-interrupt/

Rapport: An unconscious empathetic relationship to another person based on mutual trust, understanding, and respect.

https://excellenceassured.com/nlp-training/nlp-certification/rapport

Shock Value: The potential of an image, text, action, or other form of communication to provoke a sharp negative reaction.

https://en.wikipedia.org/wiki/Shock_value

Social Proof: A concept stating that people tend to do what others are doing
https://www.transformdestiny.com/nlp-blog/the-power-of-social-proof/

Michael Brackman

Trance: A half-conscious state in which there is a lack of response to external factors or stimuli.

https://jamespesch.com/hypnosis-trance-meditation-nlp-does-it-work/

Transferring: Carrying the authority or prestige of something respected over to something else in order to make it acceptable. Inversely, carrying over disapproval to influence others to reject or disapprove of it.

Rosenberry, Jack, and Lauren A. Vicker. Applied Mass Communication Theory: A Guide for Media Practitioners. Routledge, Taylor & Francis Group, 2017.

Reference List

Chapter 2

Cohn pure EVIL Vanity Fair
https://www.vanityfair.com/news/2017/06/ donald-trump-roy-cohn-relationship

"Donald pisses ice water"

Trump: The Deals and the Downfall, Wayne Barrett (1992)

https://theweek.com/speedreads/617343/d onald-trump-turned-back-closest-friend- when-heard-aids

Chapter 3

Trump Has Made a 10,000 False Claims

https://www.washingtonpost.com/politics/2 019/04/29/president-trump-has-made- more-than-false-or-misleading-claims/?noredirect=on&utm_term=.6b8cafd b3657

Chapter 4

Rust Interview

https://www.wircd.com/story/the-man- who-saw-the-dangers-of-cambridge- analytica/

Data Propria Mention

https://qz.com/1307531/scandal-ridden- cambridge-analytica-is-gone-but-its-staffers- are-hard-at-work-again/

Bannon Quote

https://www.sltrib.com/opinion/commentar y/2018/02/09/michael-lewis-looking-for- trump-in-all-the-wrong-places/

Picture of Trump in Meeting

https://www.gettyimages.com/detail/news-photo/president-donald-trump-argues-about-border-security-with-news-photo/1071834200?adppopup=true

INDEX

achiever, 14, 15, 16, 17
Adolf Hitler, 70
Aleksander Kogan, 23
Anchoring, 29
Barrett's 1992 book about Trump, 11
Ben Taub, 66
Cambridge Analytica, 13, 23, 24, 25, 26, 27, 28, 33, 53, 65
Chosen Ones, 25
Colin Kaepernick, 13
Data Propria, 28
Don Lemon, 65, 85
Dr. Richard Bandler, 95
Enneagram, 14, 16
Ericksonian, 1, 55
Friedrich Blumenbach, 70
Friedrich Trump, 37
Hassan Rouhani, 67
Horst Rechelbacher, 74
Howard Stern, 7, 64, 81, 91
Hypnosis, 22, 26, 55
Ivana Trump, 12
James Comey's, 7
Jared Kushner, 25
Jim Jones, 65
John Grinder, 18
Keith Raniere, 55
Kim Jong-un, 68, 80
MAGA, 53
Make America Great Again, 53
Marianne Williamson, 89
Marla Maples, 12
McCarthyism, 10

Michael D'Antonio, 37
Milton Model, 19
mirroring, 19, 97
Mueller Report, 32
Nancy Zulsman, 55
neuro-linguistic programming, 1
Nigel Oakes, 23
Nipsey Hussle, 83
NLP, 1, 18, 19, 20, 23, 55, 94, 95
NXIVM, 55, 58
Obama, 54
Oprah, 91, 95
Paul McKenna, 99
Pavlov, 29, 79
Peter Fraser, 11
Politico, 57
Prince, 84
Psychometrics Center, 24
Repetition, 52
Robert Dilts, 19
Roy Cohn, 10
SHEEPLE, 1
shock value, 31, 99
Steve Bannon, 26
Strategic Communications Laboratories, 23
TED Talk, 78
The Art of the Deal, 37
Tim Albert, 35
Trumpnosis, 7, 1, 3, 4
Trumpnosis Patterns, 3

TRUMP CAN WIN IN 2020

www.ingramcontent.com/pod-product-compliance
Lightning Source LLC
Chambersburg PA
CBHW071514040426
42444CB00008B/1648